Second

Titles in the Harvestime **Pressure Points** series:

Don't Call Me Chicken—Peggy Burns
Far Side of the Shadow—Peggy Burns
Hands Off!—Roger Day
Henrietta Pudding—Peggy Burns
Hard Sell—Roger Day
The Web—Peggy Burns
Breaking Out—Liz Priestley
Dead Cert—Roger Day
Second Best—Eunice Davies

Second Best

Eunice Davies

Illustrations: Liz Priestley

Harvestime

Published in the United Kingdom by:
Harvestime Services Ltd, 136 Hall Lane, Bradford
West Yorkshire BD4 7DG

First published by Harvestime
First printed March 1988

British Library Cataloguing in Publication Data

Davies, Eunice
Second best.
I. Title II. Priestley, Liz III. Series
823'.914 [J]

ISBN 0-947714-46-4

Typeset by in the United Kingdom by:
Grassroots Limited, London N3 2LJ
Printed and bound in the United Kingdom by:
Richard Clay Ltd., Bungay, Suffolk

Contents

1

Piggy-in-the-middle

One of the boys at the bus stop caught sight of Jane. He nudged his friends and tipped his head in her direction.

'Hey—Olive Oyl! How's Popeye?' he shouted. 'Slipped down any good drains lately, Sparrow-legs?'

The girl kept walking. She turned her head away as her face went crimson. 'Boys are the pits,' she muttered as she hurried round the corner.

Jane lived in a terrace house behind the park, and as she turned into her street she saw her older sister, Diane, climbing the park wall. When Diane spotted Jane she stood on top of the wall waving her tennis-racket.

'Fancy a game, Janey?' she called.

'What about tea?' Jane replied crossly. 'Mum's working late and we need to get started. There's no time for games of tennis.'

Diane jumped down into the park and walked away, swinging her tennis-racket in the air as if she was serving a ball. 'Tea can wait. I want a game of tennis,' she called over her shoulder.

Jane went into the house feeling angry. Diane and her precious tennis! Whenever there were any jobs to be done around the house, you could be sure there would be a game of some sort her sister wanted to play!

As she passed through the large kitchen, Jane glanced at the breakfast remains that still littered the table—dirty cutlery, sticky dishes and cereal packets.

Hanging up her coat she called, 'Jeremy Spencer—are you watching telly? You haven't tidied the breakfast things away.' She went into the sitting-room and drew the curtains that had been left closed from the previous night.

'Are you deaf?' she shouted.

'No, I'm not deaf. Mum won't be home till six, so get lost. I'm watching this programme. There's plenty of time to do the washing-up. If you want it done now, do it yourself!' He turned up the sound using the remote control and pulled a face at his sister.

Jeremy was a very stubborn ten-year-old and Jane wasn't in the mood for a pitched battle.

She went up to the room she shared with Diane. As she passed Jeremy's bedroom, she glanced in. A pair of very muddy football boots were in the doorway and the floor was littered with PE kit, comics, crisp and sweet packets and drawings of assorted shapes and sizes.

Jane hated untidiness and she was tempted to go in and sort it out, but she didn't. Why should she? Her brother was a lazy lout and if he wanted to live in a pigsty, why should she care?

Once in her room, she lay on the bed staring at the ceiling. She'd had a rotten day and she felt angry and frustrated.

Mr Adams, the maths teacher, had shouted at her because she couldn't do the work he'd set them.

Her best friend had gone off with somebody else—and that had really hurt. Mandy wasn't such a fantastic friend, but she was the only one Jane had.

Those stupid boys at the bus stop had called her Olive Oyl because she was thin. Now her family were being as selfish and obnoxious as usual!

She had a pretty, older sister who sailed through her school work without a single problem. Diane's hair was wavy and blonde. She had a spot-free complexion, not to mention gorgeous legs. She was brilliant at sport, popular with everybody, and Daddy's darling.

Mum was always tired and irritable, with no time to notice how others were feeling. And there was spoilt little Jeremy, who according to his mother was a future artistic genius who had to be kept happy at all costs because of his artistic temperament and asthma attacks.

Jane flicked her radio to Radio One and reached for her magnifying mirror. Unlike her sister, she had problems with her complexion. She lay gazing at her nose. She'd tried everything from nightly scrubbing to lotions, but her nose was still greasy and full of blackheads.

She threw the mirror down and began to examine her nails. She'd bitten them since she was seven and hated herself for it. Jane made yet another resolution to leave her nails alone. As she lay there she decided, once again, to have early nights and not to read until the early hours of the morning.

Suddenly, she heard the front door bang. That sounded like Dad! She jumped up and switched off the radio.

'Jane!' he shouted. 'What's going on? Have you seen this mess?'

Jane hurried downstairs. Whenever her father was in the house she felt nervy and on edge. He was a great shouter and slammer of doors—and had been known to throw things when he was angry. Diane and Jeremy didn't seem to be affected by Mr Spencer's tantrums, but Jane hated them.

'Coming, Dad,' she called. Hurrying into the kitchen she began to clear the breakfast things away.

'I want a meal on the table before your mum comes home. What have you been playing at?' Mr Spencer said crossly.

'Jeremy should have cleared these. Breakfast is his job,' Jane told him.

'He's not feeling too good,' her dad replied.

'And Diane should be here to help. She's playing tennis on the park court.'

'Don't stand there wasting time talking and making excuses—just get on with it. Where's my paper?'

Jane wanted to kick something. It was always the same. She felt like piggy-in-the-middle. It wasn't fair.

The sausages and mash were ready when Diane came back from her game of tennis.

'I'm starving,' she said as she walked in. She began setting the table. 'Do we need spoons? Are we having pudding, Janey?'

'You tell me. And don't call me Janey.' Jane glared at her sister.

'Pardon me for living,' Diane replied.

'Why don't *you* make pudding if you want it. I've had to clear the breakfast things, peel potatoes and grill sausages while you were playing your precious game.'

Diane sighed. 'Not another pity-party! I'm helping now, aren't I? I told you to wait—it's your own fault.'

'Dad came home and wanted things to get moving,' Jane snapped.

Diane laughed. 'Big deal,' she said.

Mrs Spencer arrived home looking even more tired and

harassed than usual. Jeremy tried to look ill when Jane complained that he hadn't cleared the breakfast things.

Mr Spencer propped his newspaper up against the tomato-ketchup bottle and ignored everyone. Jane was near to tears and found it difficult to swallow because she felt badly done-to. Diane talked constantly about the forthcoming tennis tournament.

After the meal Mrs Spencer began to tidy, dust and vacuum the house. She worked full-time and had to do the housework in the evenings and at weekends. The rest of the family dreaded Friday evenings and usually went out.

'I'm off to the disco, Mum,' Diane shouted over the noise of the vacuum cleaner.

'It's all right for some! I hope you've left your room tidy so I can clean it,' Mrs Spencer shouted, but Diane had gone.

Jeremy was out on his bike and Jane was attempting to do her maths homework. The noise of her mother's cleaning didn't help her concentration, or the headache which had come on during tea. Jane wished *she* had somewhere to go. She had arranged to go to the cinema with Mandy—but now Mandy wasn't her friend anymore.

Flinging her maths book on to the bed, Jane picked up a novel. She was reading Emily Brontë's *Wuthering Heights* for the third time. She enjoyed sad, tragic books—and sometimes read them under the bedcovers with a torch late at night. Often she cried herself to sleep as she reread her favourite weepy bits.

Her mother came in. Mrs Spencer was feeling worn out. 'Charming!' she exclaimed. 'I'm working like a charlady—and I find her ladyship with her feet up, reading a book!'

She tutted and sighed as she bustled around the room,

dusting. Jane sat up, feeling guilty. Why did her mother have to work full-time? There might be more money, but Mum seemed to be permanently tired and depressed!

Jane's headache pounded in her temples and her stomach was a tight knot of frustration and anger.

Mrs Spencer looked out of the window as she heard the sound of the front gate opening.

'Someone's coming to the door, Jane. Is it too much trouble for you to go and see what they want?'

Jane was thankful to get out of the room. The doorbell rang as she ran downstairs.

A boy about her own age was standing on the step. He was tall and good looking. He smiled.

'We've just moved in over the road and we can't find the tap that turns the water on. We wondered if you could help?'

Feeling shy and self-conscious, Jane told him where to find the tap. She wished she'd combed her hair before answering the door. She also had on her school uniform. Horrors!

'Thanks. My name's David, by the way,' the boy said in a friendly way as he turned and went down the path.

'I'm Jane Spencer,' Jane told him timidly.

'See you around, Jane.'

Jane closed the door. He was nice. He had dark hair and light blue eyes—an attractive combination. And he had a pleasant way of speaking, too.

'Who was it?' Mrs Spencer called as she came downstairs carrying the vacuum cleaner.

'Our new neighbour from number nine,' Jane replied, dreamily.

She went slowly upstairs, deciding to have a shower and an early night. Maybe she'd use one of Mum's face packs.

Later, when Jane was reading in her room, Diane came in.

'Hi, young sis. Fantastic disco! It was brill!'

She got undressed, dropping her clothes on the floor, then leapt into bed.

'You should come with me—you never go anywhere these days, Janey.' Diane snuggled down under her blankets. 'Let's have the light off,' she said. 'I have to be up early in the morning. Tennis practice. Then we're going ice-skating.'

With a sigh, Jane turned out the light. It was true that she never went anywhere. Diane was always out—she loved sport and had lots of friends.

Ice-skating. Jane groaned quietly when she remembered the time years ago when Mr Spencer had taken his two daughters to the ice-rink. Jane had been hopeless, clinging to the side for dear life. Her dad had soon lost patience and left her there. Diane had been an instant success as usual.

She sighed again and turned over. *Let's face it,* she thought. *I'm second best in this family.*

And who wanted second best? Nobody! Plain Jane—that was her!

Jane felt under the pillow for her torch and book. She wanted to read the sad parts again.

Somehow it helped. Having a good cry made the tight, tense, unhappy feeling go away—though Jane knew it would be back tomorrow.

2

Wire wool

'Get up at once!' Mr Spencer yelled. Jane nearly jumped out of her skin. She sat up in bed, head throbbing and eyes aching.

'Do you realise it's past eleven o'clock? I thought you'd gone into hibernation!' He went out of the room, slamming the bedroom door so hard the windows rattled. Jane winced.

Shakily, she got dressed and went to the bathroom. Dad always seemed to be in a bad mood on Saturday mornings and Jane usually got the worst of it. Mum went out to do the shopping and Jeremy was usually out with his friends at the swimming-baths. Diane was inevitably up early playing some game or other.

Jane hurried downstairs. Her dad was reading the paper in the kitchen. The room seemed like a bomb site.

'You look terrible, my girl. What's wrong with you? You never go anywhere or do anything—but you always look as if you've had a night on the tiles,' Mr Spencer said unkindly.

'I couldn't get to sleep last night, that's all,' Jane answered tearfully. 'I've got a rotten headache, if you must know.' She began to tidy the kitchen.

'Don't turn on the waterworks, Jane—I'm not in the mood. It's time you pulled yourself together. Be like Diane! You don't catch *her* lying around in bed. She's out in the fresh air playing games and keeping fit.' Dad folded his newspaper vigorously.

'I don't like sport,' Jane answered as the tears began to flow. 'Leave me alone, can't you?'

'I'll leave you alone all right—and so will everybody else if you go around looking like a dying duck in a thunderstorm.' Mr Spencer stood up to leave.

'I'm going to the pub for an hour. When I get back I expect to see this kitchen sorted out,' he growled as he left.

Jane tidied the kitchen and had some toast and a cup of tea. She searched for some paracetamol for her headache, which had grown worse with crying. When her mother came back with the shopping, Jane helped her put it all away.

'Fish and chips for lunch, Jane,' her mother said. 'Do some bread and butter.' Mrs Spencer put her feet up and had a cup of coffee. 'It's like a battleground in that supermarket, pushing, shoving and queuing for hours.'

Jane's stomach quaked at the thought of fish and chips yet again. They were always having them.

Her mother looked at her. 'Have you been crying?' she asked. 'You look awful.'

'I'm all right. I've got a rotten headache, and I don't want fish and chips. When I've buttered this bread I think I'll ring Mandy. We might go down town.'

Mandy had walked off the day before with two other girls, but it was worth a try. Jane just wanted to get out of the house.

'Well, for goodness' sake wash your hair before you go

anywhere. It looks like rats' tails,' her mother called as Jane went to the telephone.

Jane looked at herself in the hall mirror. Her eyes were bloodshot from reading until two in the morning and her hair was greasy and lank. She turned away and dialled Mandy's number.

The phone rang for a long time before Mandy's tired voice said, 'Hello.'

'It's me—Jane. Doing anything this afternoon?' Jane asked tentatively.

'I was doing something when you rang—*sleeping!*' Mandy said sarcastically.

'Sorry,' Jane apologised. 'But it *is* half-past twelve.'

'So what? It's Saturday, isn't it? I was out late last night. I always stay in bed on Saturday mornings.'

'Sorry,' Jane repeated. 'I fancied a trip to town, but I didn't know whether you'd still be interested, after yesterday.'

Mandy sighed. 'Yeah, well . . . sorry about that. I'm glad you rang. Look, I'll see you in the shopping precinct at half past two.'

Jane washed her hair and was drying it as Diane breezed in, her blonde curls bouncing and shining with health. Jane stared at her sister's hair.

'Why was I the one to get the straight mousy hair and you got blonde curls?' she asked bitterly.

'Don't start another pity-party, Janey. Anybody can have blonde curls. Just have it dyed and permed!' Diane flung herself on to the bed. 'I'm starving!' she declared. 'I hope it's fish and chips for lunch.'

'What a brilliant idea!' Jane said enthusiastically.

Diane frowned. 'I thought you weren't keen on fish and chips.'

'Not the fish and chips, idiot—my hair! I never thought of having it dyed and permed.'

Diane stood up. 'Well, it's only a good idea if you have it done at a decent hairdresser's. It'll cost you. Don't have it done on the cheap or you'll be sorry.'

* * *

By the time she met Mandy in the shopping precinct, Jane had made up her mind. She *would* have her hair dyed and permed. Somehow she'd get the money.

Mandy was all for it. 'Anything for a laugh,' she giggled. Mandy was a notorious giggler. To Jane's embarrassment she giggled her way in and out of a dozen hairdressers' shops as they went around asking prices.

It was very expensive wherever they went. Jane began to lose hope that she'd ever be able to afford to have her hair done. Then Mandy made a suggestion.

'It's these posh shops in the town centre that are expensive. Let's go to that little place around the corner from our house. I bet that'll be cheaper.'

It was cheaper, and Jane made an appointment for the following week, deciding she'd pay for it somehow.

During the next few days she tried to get the money together. Her mother thought it was a crazy idea, but she gave Jane enough to have a decent haircut. Diane lent her two pounds. Jeremy, the ten-year-old miser, simply told her to get lost. Jane wasn't desperate enough to ask *Dad* for extra money.

Money was one of Mr Spencer's chief moans. He could go on for hours complaining about electricity bills when lights were left on. The telephone bill was always a disaster and he never paid for anything without a complaint.

Jane did some babysitting for neighbours. Then, by asking for her spending money early, she managed to get enough to pay for her hair. She was very excited and lingered for a long time in front of mirrors trying to imagine her head covered in soft golden curls.

As she set off to the hairdresser's she met David, their new neighbour. He asked if she knew where the nearest cycle shop was, then walked with her to the bus stop.

She felt awkward and shy. David was relaxed and friendly and did most of the talking. He told her he'd be starting at her school the following Monday.

'See you again, Jane,' he called as she climbed on to the bus.

Jane wished she had Diane's self-confidence when talking to boys. Her mind always went blank! She seemed to say the dumbest things, especially when the boy was as nice as David. Once on the bus, she could think of a dozen amusing and interesting things she could have said to him.

As she went into the little shop she had butterflies in her stomach. The hairdresser seemed bored and asked Jane questions in a disinterested tone of voice. She chewed gum vigorously and noisily.

'How much do you want off?'

Jane wasn't sure.

'Do you want highlights all over or just at the front? Do you want a top-perm or a full-head?'

Jane wasn't sure what she wanted and began to feel apprehensive. The girl didn't exactly fill her with confidence. Jane needed advice but the hairdresser said, 'It's just up to you, love.'

They finally got started, and it seemed to take hours. Peculiar-smelling lotions, curlers with little pieces of tissue and hot dryers.

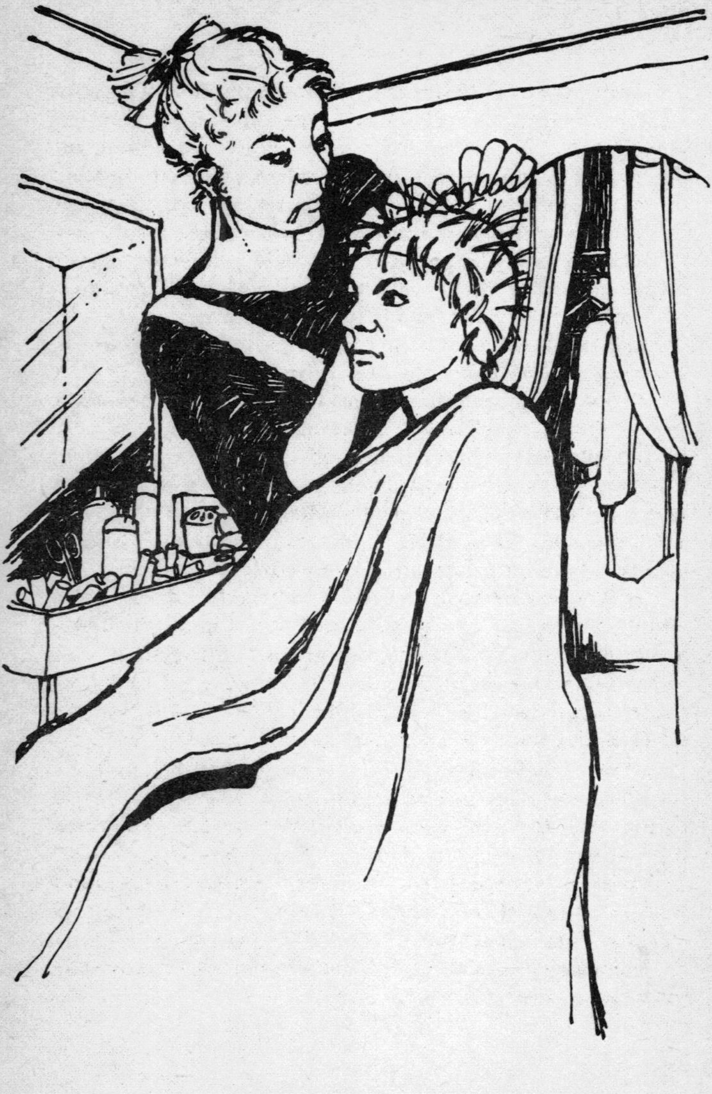

At one stage she had to have a very tight-fitting cap on. The hairdresser then pulled tufts of Jane's hair through with a hook till she looked like someone who'd just had an electric shock. She was relieved that Mandy wasn't around, otherwise it would have been one long giggle.

When they were about halfway through, a paper-boy came in to leave the evening paper. He winked at Jane, and with horror she recognised Shaun McSpadden, who was in her form at school.

He'd never let her live this down! Her heart sank as she looked at herself, covered in bright pink curlers. With a plastic bag on her head she looked a sight—and Shaun McSpadden would make sure everybody knew all the details on Monday morning!

When the hair was finished it was certainly blonde and curly—but not at all how Jane had imagined it would be. It wasn't shiny. It looked dull and wiry—more crinkly than curly. It was too short and her ears stuck out.

Panic welled up inside her. What had she done? It was awful. She hardly heard what the hairdresser was saying as she paid her money and rushed out of the shop.

Jane talked to herself as she hurried along. 'Oh, no,' she whispered as she saw her reflection in a shop window. 'It looks like wire wool! Please don't let me meet anybody I know!'

What was she going to do? She'd never been so miserable! On the bus she hung her head wishing she had a hood or a scarf.

As she turned into her road, Jeremy was cycling around with two friends. She wanted the ground to open up and swallow her, but it didn't.

'Woo! Fizzy-bonce!' Jeremy called as he cycled alongside his sister.

'Drop dead!' Jane snapped. She ran on, head down—and bumped straight into someone. She stared into David's smiling face. He opened his mouth to speak, but Jane gave a little scream and ran across the road. The front path seemed two miles long. Finally, she shot through the door, banging it shut.

'Don't slam that door!' her father barked from the lounge. 'How many times do I have to tell you kids?'

Jane burst into tears. 'Oh—shut up!' she screamed, running upstairs. She slammed the bedroom door as hard as she could and threw herself on to her bed. Why, oh why, did nothing ever go right for her?

'I wish I was dead,' she sobbed, burying her face in her pillow. 'Oh—I wish I was dead!'

And she found she really meant it.

3

A willing slave

'Jane Spencer, where's your homework?' Mr Adams demanded. 'What's the matter with you, girl? You look half asleep!'

'I didn't do the homework because I was away on Monday, sir,' Jane answered timidly. Mr Adams scared her and she had great difficulty understanding what he was talking about most of the time.

'You know you're lagging behind, don't you? It's the exams in three weeks!' He shrugged his shoulders.

He stood up and turned to the blackboard. His voice droned on and the chalk squeaked on the board. Jane tried hard to concentrate, but she felt so tired.

There'd been a family row going on for most of the weekend. It had started when she'd told her father to shut up. Because of the row, the tears and the lack of sleep, her Mum had allowed her to stay at home on Monday and Tuesday.

'So, Jane Spencer—how can I find out how long this line is?'

Hearing her name, Jane jumped and stared at Mr Adams.

'Well, come on. I've just spent the last ten minutes telling you how to do it!' Mr Adams banged on the blackboard with the chalk. He drew a circle round some figures.

'Have you got anything between your ears, girl? What does this mean?'

Jane found maths difficult, but when Mr Adams shouted, it was ten times worse.

'Will you answer me—what does this mean?' He banged again with the chalk. Jane felt herself going red and her heart was beating very fast.

'Have you been listening, Jane?'

'Yes, sir,' she murmured. She felt tears stinging her eyes. Just then the bell rang, echoing through the school, announcing the end of the lesson.

Mandy and Jane walked to their next lesson.

'Adams Apple is a real pig,' Mandy commented sympathetically.

Jane nodded, feeling comforted. Next lesson was art with Mr Pollard. Everyone called him Pansy Pollard, but Jane liked him. He never got angry, nor did he ever shout.

Art was easy and undemanding. The lessons were usually chaotic—order and organisation weren't exactly Mr Pollard's strong points. He praised everyone and was always satisfied, even when people obviously hadn't tried their best.

The project for the day was buttercups. Arranged around the room, in various jamjars and pots, were yellow buttercups.

Much to Jane's dismay, she ended up sitting in front of Shaun McSpadden.

'Sir—can I draw Jane Spencer's hair instead of the flowers?' he shouted. 'It's more interesting!'

Mandy turned round and said something rude to him, but he continued.

'Seventy-six pink rollers on Jane Spencer's head,' he sang to a well-known tune.

'You'll have a *jamjar* on your head in a minute, McSpadden, if you don't cool it,' Mandy snarled.

'Lost your tongue, Spencer?' Shaun went on, laughing. 'That plastic bag you were wearing probably did something nasty to your brain.'

'Now come on, Shaun,' Mr Pollard called. 'You're one of my best artists. Let's have some work done.'

Jane went over to the teacher's desk to sharpen her pencil. Mr Pollard looked at her and said, 'Are you all right, Jane?'

'Yes sir. But I've got a headache,' she replied quietly. She thought Mr Pollard was wonderful. So kind and thoughtful—not like most men she knew.

'Go and get some paracetamol from the nurse, and then perhaps you'd like to sit in the library. Or you could tidy the storeroom,' he said, smiling.

Jane spent a lot of time helping to keep the Art Room tidy. She was an expert at tidying up and enjoyed cleaning sinks and brushes.

'I'll do the storeroom, sir, please,' Jane whispered.

'Thanks, Jane. That'll be a help—and at least it's peaceful in there,' Mr Pollard replied, glancing towards Shaun McSpadden, who was now annoying someone else.

Jane spent the remainder of the lesson in the storeroom bringing order from the chaos she found there. As the lesson finished, Shaun McSpadden called through the door, 'Where's the wire-haired poodle gone? Ah—there she is, doing tricks for Pansy!'

Jane pretended to ignore him, but blushed a bright red.

She began to clean the sink. She was in no hurry to go for lunch; Mandy would be at her band practice.

Soon the storeroom was looking spick and span. Mr Pollard would be pleased. There was nobody about and Jane decided to eat her sandwiches in the storeroom.

It was nice and peaceful. The dining-room was very noisy: trays banging, chairs scraping on the floor, dinner ladies shouting and hundreds of kids talking at the tops of their voices.

After a while Mandy came into the classroom looking for Jane.

'Why are you still here?' she asked as she walked into the storeroom and perched on the corner of a box. 'Did Pansy say you could have your sandwiches in here?'

'Don't call him Pansy. It's not nice,' Jane said. 'What's the Junior Brass Band been up to?' she continued, trying to change the subject.

'Well!' Mandy said putting her feet up and looking very pleased with herself. 'There's this new lad—he's fantastic! Plays the cornet like a dream. He sat next to me and we shared a music-stand. Really handsome and friendly. I think he liked me. He's a fourth year but looks like a sixth former. He's dead dishy.' Mandy sighed. 'We talked for ages.'

She stirred restlessly. 'I think I might wander, if you're staying here—I could just meet my cornet player again. See you.'

Jane shook her head. Mandy and her crushes! They happened at regular intervals, but nothing ever came of them. Once she'd even admired Shaun McSpadden from afar until he'd called her 'Freckles'. That had been the end of a fine romance before it had even begun!

Jane sighed, thinking of Mr Pollard. Raymond George

Pollard. Ray was a nice name, she thought. She went into the classroom and began tidying up after the buttercup session. She talked to herself, pretending she was addressing Mr Pollard. She imagined a secret meeting between them. She was sure he liked her.

She was putting the unused paper in the storeroom when she heard someone come into the classroom. Her heart jumped and her cheeks flushed. She hoped it was Mr Pollard—she might get a chance to talk to him.

She heard voices and listened. A woman was talking.

'What's happened to your room, Ray? It's always such a tip. Are you changing from a slob to a respectable art master at last?'

The man laughed. 'Sorry to disappoint you, Clare. But I've got a willing slave—a very efficient one who can tidy up in no time.'

'Who's that? Anybody I know?' It was Miss Drinkwater, the Latin mistress, who was talking to Mr Pollard.

Jane felt embarrassed and uncomfortable and thought she'd better bang about and make her presence known. But she hesitated. They were talking about her . . . . Mr Pollard might say what he thought about her.

'It's Jane Spencer from three-ten. A tall, thin kid with spots. She's just had her hair done and it looks like wire wool.'

'I know who you mean,' Miss Drinkwater replied. 'Her sister, Diane, is in my Latin group—a very attractive and bright kid.'

'That's her. Chalk and cheese, those two sisters. Jane is like a frightened, bedraggled colt, poor kid. Her art is pathetic—she's got nothing going for her at all. Diane's the opposite. Bags of confidence and talent.'

'At least Jane's capable of tidying up,' Miss Drinkwater

said, laughing. 'I must dash, Ray. See you later.'

'Yes—she's a willing and devoted slave. I'll pick you up around eight if that's OK.'

Jane heard Miss Drinkwater leaving. She stood still, not daring to move. Hurting inside. Feeling rejected. So, Mr Pollard thought she was pathetic!

She heard him leaving. She slid down in a heap in the corner, staring into space.

'Jane!' Mandy called. 'Come on—it's time for next lesson. Hey, I've seen him again, and he waved. This time it's love. Jane—are you there?'

Jane came out of the storeroom.

'What's up? Are you going to be sick?' Mandy asked. Her friend looked very pale.

'I'm all right. Don't ask. Come on—let's get out of this dump.' Jane hurried out of the Art Room, Mandy rushing to catch her up.

'If I see him I'll point him out,' Mandy whispered as they hurried along to the geography room.

'If you see who?' Jane asked, frowning.

'My cornet player, of course,' Mandy replied in a hurt voice.

'Look—there he is. Oh no! He's talking to your rotten sister! I won't stand a chance if she gets her claws into him,' Mandy hissed angrily.

Jane looked down the corridor. Diane was talking to David, the boy from across the road. He saw Jane, and gave her a smile and a quick wave.

She turned away, ignoring him, and hurried on to her geography lesson.

4

Specky Four-eyes

'Jane—stop doing that,' her mother said, crossly. 'You'll have wrinkles before you're twenty.'

Jane was absorbed in watching a film on TV. It was very sad and tragic—exactly the kind of film she enjoyed. In her imagination she was suffering with the heroine, and thoroughly enjoying it.

'Doing what?' Jane asked, her eyes still glued to the set.

'Peering, with your eyes all screwed up. Are you listening to me? Stop peering!' her mother replied.

Jane often exasperated her. Diane—who was quick at everything—had never been any trouble. And Jeremy was the son she'd always wanted. But Jane was a disappointment. Mrs Spencer often felt annoyed with her, hardly knowing the reason why.

She sighed. 'Can't you see properly, Jane? What's the matter with you?'

'See what?'

Mrs Spencer suddenly lost her temper. 'You're screwing your eyes up again! Stop it!' she shouted.

Jane jumped. She looked round at her mother, who for some reason seemed suddenly very annoyed.

'Sorry, Mum,' Jane apologised. 'The TV *is* a bit blurred. And sometimes I can't see the board at school.'

Mrs Spencer's knitting clicked on. She was frowning. Jane turned back to her film.

'You'd better have your eyes tested. You might need glasses.'

'But I don't want to wear glasses.'

'People don't wear glasses because they want to. They wear them because they have to,' Mrs Spencer replied.

Jane woke the next morning with a heavy feeling. Then she remembered: she needed glasses. She hoped her mother would forget about it.

But it wasn't to be. That evening Mr Spencer was told that Jane was short-sighted.

'You'll ruin your eyes if you don't wear glasses when you need them,' was his first comment.

'You wouldn't catch *me* in a pair of specs,' Diane exclaimed.

'I could call you "Specky Four-eyes",' Jeremy grinned.

'Shut up, little brother. And don't chew with your mouth open—it sounds disgusting,' Jane snapped.

Mrs Spencer turned on Jane. 'Don't pick on Jeremy because you need glasses, my girl.'

'The subject is closed,' growled Dad. 'Make an appointment at the optician's. If you need glasses you'll have to wear glasses—and that's final.'

Jane found the prospect of going to an optician even worse than a visit to the dentist. She went with Mandy, who sat in the waiting-room reading leaflets about glasses.

Jane was tense and nervous in spite of the optician's relaxed, friendly manner. She screwed her eyes up as she tried to read the letters on the wall-chart. The bottom lines were simply too small.

Then the optician fitted a cumbersome contraption, like a huge, ugly pair of glasses, in front of her eyes. He asked her to read a line on the chart, trying different lenses. After a while, the letters began to look amazingly clear.

Then he shone a bright light into her eyes and inspected them closely.

It seemed to take for ever, and when he had finished his examination the optician told her she was short-sighted—as she had expected.

On her way out, Jane arranged to come back with her mother to choose a pair of frames that suited her. Her eyes were her only good point, Jane felt—large, dark and long-lashed. Now they were about to be hidden behind glass that would make them look smaller.

It was a relief to get out into the street.

'I'll only need to wear them at home and when I can't see the blackboard,' Jane told Mandy.

'I wouldn't wear them at all,' said Mandy fiercely. 'I'd get contact lenses. My brother, Oliver, has a pair, and they're great—you can't tell he's wearing them. Mind you, having to stick something into your eyes every morning is a bit off-putting, but anything's better than wearing glasses.'

'Contact lenses!' Jane exclaimed. 'Why didn't I think of that? That's the answer!' They returned to the shop and collected a leaflet which explained all about them.

Jane told her Mum about the lenses. She felt better already.

'You can't see them at all, and they don't hurt once you get used to them,' she said excitedly.

Mrs Spencer looked at the leaflet. 'They'll cost the earth—*and* they have to be insured. A woman where I work bought a pair. She paid a fortune, then found she couldn't wear them.'

'They do cost more than glasses, but I think they're supposed to last longer,' Jane replied positively, though feeling her confidence diminishing.

Later, it disappeared altogether when her father gave a five-minute lecture on the cost of living.

'When you're earning money, you can buy yourself some,' he concluded. 'It's bad enough having to pay a bill for glasses—but contact lenses. No way can we afford that! At least we're not making you wear National Health frames.'

Jane's hopes were dashed. She spent the next few days looking at people who wore glasses, and she had to admit that some people looked good in them. One of the PE teachers wore a large, bright-blue pair, and she looked very attractive.

The following Saturday she went with her mother to choose a pair of frames. Jane had wanted Mandy to come along, but Mrs Spencer said she couldn't stand Mandy and her silly giggling.

The optician's wall held a vast array of spectacle frames, attractively displayed with bright lights and lots of mirrors. However, when Mrs Spencer told the assistant how much they wanted to spend, it cut the choice down quite a lot.

Jane felt unsure of herself, and her insecurity increased with every pair she tried on. Some of the frames looked huge and heavy. Others made her look like an owl. As she peered into the mirror she seemed to be gazing at a stranger.

Mrs Spencer began to feel irritated by her daughter's indecision.

'Come on, Jane. You must like *one* pair out of all these! I can't stay here all afternoon while you try glasses on.

Now, choose a pair and let's go. I've got a lot of shopping to do.'

Jane panicked. She didn't like any of them. She felt near to tears.

'I just don't feel right in them. I wish I could have contact lenses. They're . . . .'

'Well, you can't,' Mrs Spencer interrupted. 'So get on and make up your mind.'

A pair was chosen and ordered and Jane went off to meet Mandy, leaving Mrs Spencer to do some shopping.

'Well, what are they like, then?' Mandy asked as soon as she saw her friend.

'Blue. They're OK, I suppose,' Jane replied with a heavy heart.

'Blue and OK. That's not a very enthusiastic description.'

'I don't feel very enthusiastic. I'm cheesed off with the whole subject. I don't want to talk about it,' Jane said bitterly.

'Well, don't take it out on me. It's not my fault. Come on—let's try hats on in this store. Anything for a laugh.' Mandy took her friend's arm and led her into the store.

Later, Jane decided she would begin to save up for some contact lenses. She realised it would take her a long time. Maybe she could put a card in the paper-shop window offering her services as a babysitter.

On the way home from school the following day she met David and they walked together up the street. As they came to his gate, he said, 'Would you like to come ice-skating with us on Friday? There's a group of young people going from my church, and we're inviting friends.'

Jane blushed. She couldn't believe her ears. But was he just trying to be friendly in order to get near Diane?

'I'm hopeless at skating,' she said abruptly, and walked off.

When she got into the house she wanted to kick herself. Why was she like that? Why couldn't she be friendly to David? He really was nice.

She stood in the hall and looked at her reflection in the mirror, trying to visualise herself in the blue glasses. What would David think about them? How she wished Dad could afford contact lenses!

Diane came through the door and nearly bumped into her.

'Why are you looking down in the dumps?' she asked.

'I'm all right,' Jane replied.

'I'll be all right, too, if I can only get Dad to say I can go with the school on the five-day trip to Paris,' Diane said as she charged upstairs. Jane followed more slowly.

'You've a hope!' Jane remarked, coming into the bedroom.

'I can get round Dad. Don't you worry,' Diane replied confidently.

5

'Nobody cares'

'Jeremy! Get your hand out of the cornflake packet. What do you think you're doing? If I know your hand, it won't be very clean!'

Jane snatched the cornflake packet and the flakes cascaded over the kitchen floor.

'You idiot!' Jeremy shouted. 'You knocked 'em down—so you sweep 'em up!'

Jane went to get the dustpan and brush. 'It was your fault. You had your hand in them,' Jane complained.

Mr Spencer walked in looking at his newspaper and crunched through the cornflakes. He didn't have his shoes on and they stuck to his socks.

'What are you playing at, Jane?' he demanded accusingly.

'It wasn't me.' Jane bent down and began to sweep. 'It's your precious son and his unhygienic tricks. He had his hand in them. I tried to rescue them—and he threw them all over the floor.'

'Rubbish. She snatched them, Dad,' Jeremy said, pulling a face at Jane.

'Brush my feet, Jane. I can't get these blasted flakes off

my socks.' Mr Spencer was annoyed. He was usually bad-tempered in the morning and walking through cornflakes hadn't sweetened him up.

Jeremy leaned forward and pinched Jane's bottom. She lashed out at him and sent the full bottle of milk crashing to the floor. It exploded, spraying its contents everywhere. The cornflakes and Mr Spencer's socks were well covered.

'Charming!' he shouted, jumping up. 'Why do I have idiots for children?' He pulled off his socks and threw them into the sink. 'When I can have my breakfast in peace and this mess is cleaned up, let me know.'

He tiptoed out of the room clutching his soggy newspaper.

'Jeremy—get the cloth while I pick up this glass,' Jane snapped.

'Cleaning floors is women's work,' was her brother's reply. 'If we sprinkled sugar over it all we could eat it instead!'

'Very funny. If you're not going to do anything except crack silly jokes, make yourself scarce, little brother.'

'Speaking of jokes,' Jeremy said enthusiastically, 'how do you get four elephants in a red Metro?'

'I don't know and I don't care. Mind that broken glass.'

'You get two in the front and two in the back, of course.'

Jane swept up all the glass. 'Two what?' she asked.

'Two elephants,' Jeremy replied. 'The trouble with you, Jane, is that you're a misery-guts and don't appreciate good jokes when you hear them. Typical soppy girl.'

'Jeremy—get lost.' Jane was exasperated.

'How do you know that four elephants are at the Chinese takeaway?' Jeremy persisted. Jane continued cleaning up.

'Come on, Jane, don't be such a wet blanket. You're dying to know, really.'

'Dying to know what?'

'How you know if four elephants are at the Chinese takeaway.'

'Jeremy, you're a moron. Shift that chair.'

'OK, you give in. I'll tell you. You know because the red Metro's parked outside.'

Jeremy ran from the room as Jane threw the soggy floorcloth at him. It missed.

'Cleaning the kitchen floor at this time in the morning! You'll make someone a lovely slave one day,' Diane said as she came into the kitchen. 'Well—I told you, didn't I?' she continued smugly.

'Told me what?' Jane asked as she retrieved the floorcloth.

'Told you I could get round Dad. I'm going to Paris. Aren't there any more cornflakes?' She peered into the almost empty packet.

'He said you could go to Paris? How come? I couldn't have any contact lenses.' Jane suddenly felt hurt.

'I'll have toast instead.' Diane took a loaf of bread from the cupboard.

Jane sat down on the nearest chair, stunned.

'Don't look like a hurt little rabbit, Janey. *I* know how to get round him. Anyway, it's an educational trip. I'm not doing it for my health.'

She put a slice of bread under the grill.

'Why are Dad's smelly socks in the sink covered in soggy cornflakes?' Diane asked. But Jane had gone.

She sat on her bed, stunned. Her shoulders were hunched and she looked dejected and miserable—but inside she was seething with anger.

'It's not fair,' she spat through clenched teeth. 'Nobody in this family cares tuppence about me. I wish I'd never been born.'

She lay on the bed for a long time, staring into space.

Somehow, she'd earn the money she needed—she'd get a paper round or do some more babysitting. And the minute she could, she'd leave this rotten house and never come back.

'Oh, God,' she whispered. 'If you're there—help me!'

Later that morning her mother called her.

'Jane! Come down, will you? Mrs Smithies is here to see you.'

Jane frowned. Mrs Smithies lived further down the street. What did she want? As she combed her hair she was shocked to see what a sight she looked. Crying certainly didn't improve your appearance!

Jane liked Mrs Smithies' two little children, Peter and Laura. She always talked to them and sometimes joined in their games when she was passing their garden.

'Jane—I've seen the advert you've had in the paper-shop window for the last few weeks and I'm wondering if you're interested in babysitting for us?'

Jane blinked and looked amazed. She'd forgotten about the advert she'd put in the shop so that she could get enough money for the hairdresser's. Maybe it was just coincidence—but could it possibly be that Mrs Smithies had come along now because God was helping her?

'Peter and Laura really like you. And we wouldn't be out too late.'

Jane swallowed. 'Yes,' she said eagerly. 'I will, anytime.'

'Oh—that's great. I don't suppose you could make it this evening, could you?'

'Yes! Yes, I could, Mrs Smithies.'

'Right. I'll see you around seven. And the name's Val,

by the way.'

Jane stood staring at the closed door after Val Smithies had gone. Her mum came in from the kitchen.

'Jane, you do look a sight!' she said. 'And haven't you got anything to do? You're always hanging around like a spare part!' Mrs Spencer was in a bad mood. 'What did Mrs Smithies want?'

'She wanted me to babysit,' Jane said excitedly.

'Big deal,' was her mum's comment.

* * *

'Where are we going for our holidays this year?' Jeremy asked his dad, sitting at the other end of the tea-table. He took a mouthful of bread.

'Not Clacton again,' said Diane, buttering her slice thickly with butter. 'Now you're working, Mum, we can surely afford something a bit better than that. How about Spain? That's the place to go—hot sun and discos. Brill!'

'I don't like hot sun,' Mrs Spencer said abruptly. 'It gives me a headache. And anyway, Jeremy and I would burn.'

'So because you and Jeremy have red hair and freckles, we can never go abroad? That's pathetic!' Diane raged.

'Pathetic or not, we're not going abroad this year—so forget it, Diane,' Mr Spencer interjected, forcefully.

'I want a heated pool with diving-boards, a funfair and video arcades,' Jeremy mumbled, his mouth crammed with food.

'Don't speak with your mouth full,' Jane said. Jeremy stuck his tongue out at her. It wasn't a pretty sight.

'How about Scotland?' Jane suggested.

'That's typical of Jane,' Diane said harshly. 'Scotland!

Cold and wet and very boring.'

'I want to go somewhere where I don't have to cook meals all day,' said Mrs Spencer. 'And it needs to be somewhere with lots to do so we don't argue about where to go all the time.'

The discussion continued with raised voices and Jane was glad to creep away. She got ready to go to Val's. She didn't know why, but she felt excited about her first regular babysitting job.

And she loved it. She liked Val and her husband, Martin. There was something different about them. They told her they were going to a church meeting—Jane thought it odd that people should go on a Saturday night.

She read bedtime stories to Peter and Laura, then spent a quiet evening watching TV. Val had left her some supper on a plate—delicious chicken sandwiches and a generous piece of homemade chocolate cake.

As she rinsed her plate and cup in the kitchen she noticed a poster on the kitchen wall. It said, 'Cast all your cares on him, for he cares for you.' The 'he' must mean God, she thought.

When she got home, her mum told her they were going for their holidays to Butlin's Southcoast World at Bognor Regis. Jane wasn't exactly impressed but didn't say anything.

What was the use of arguing if you're never listened to?

6

In trouble again

Jane was sick on the grass. She just wanted to lie down and die. This was the third time they'd had to stop.

'For goodness sake, Jane! Have you finished? We're never going to get there at this rate.' Jane's mother was calling to her from the car. 'You'd better sit in the front and see if that helps.'

Mrs Spencer got out and Jane took her place.

'You look like the Phantom of the Opera,' Jeremy said, laughing, 'all white and ghastly.'

Jane didn't answer. She wanted to curl up somewhere cool and quiet, away from cars and travelling and as far as possible from her horrible brother.

'Why didn't you take a travel-sickness pill, you stupid girl?' Mr Spencer said, manoeuvring the car back into the heavy traffic.

Again Jane didn't answer. She wanted to be left alone. It would have been all right by her if they'd left her on the grass verge! Who wanted to go to rotten Butlin's anyway?

Jane was much better in the front seat, and when they stopped for a picnic lunch she had a nap. It seemed to take for ever to get to Bognor. There were a lot of traffic hold-ups, and everyone became hot, tired and irritable.

Southcoast World immediately made them all feel better. It looked attractive and inviting as they arrived in the evening sunshine.

Diane and Jeremy were soon changed and ready to explore. Jane went to lie on her bunk. She quickly fell asleep but was awakened by raised voices. Her parents were arguing.

'I work hard all year, and I want a break, too,' her mum was shouting in a shrill voice.

'You agreed to come here, didn't you?' Dad shouted back. 'The kids'll be off our hands, the entertainments are all free and we can eat out some days. But not *every* day—it's too expensive and you know it!'

'So I have to shop and cook and wash-up every day? Some holiday this'll be for me! You said we'd eat out.' Mrs Spencer was angry and tearful.

'You've got two daughters to help you! And I'll help, too,' her husband replied.

Jane got up. They were always arguing, usually about housework or money. She washed her face. She still looked pale, but she felt much better and was starving hungry.

The argument continued in the next room. Now her mum was dragging up incidents from previous family holidays.

Jane sighed. It sounded like the beginning of a long row which just might last for the whole two weeks. She slipped out into the lovely summer evening, deciding she would look at the sea and then get something to eat.

'It's brill,' Diane said later as they lay on their bunks.

Jane was more relaxed about it. She hadn't wanted to come, but she had to admit the beach was superb and there was lots to do.

'Discos every night, swimming and tennis every day, and to finish it all off, a gorgeous tan,' sighed Diane. 'And tomorrow,' she continued determinedly, 'I'm taking my little sister in hand.'

'What *do* you mean?' Jane asked drowsily.

'I'm going to do something about your ghastly hair for a start—then your clothes and your make-up. I'm not going around with you as you are—we'll never get any boys.'

'I don't want any boys, thank you,' said Jane.

'Well, I do, and you and I are stuck with each other. So go to sleep and leave everything to me,' Diane added.

During the next few days the sun shone. Jeremy swam in the sea and swimming pools and played on the funfair from morning till night. Diane, with Jane trailing on behind, rushed from one activity to another during the day and danced in the disco till midnight.

Mr and Mrs Spencer spent two days shouting at one another, then lapsed into a strained silence. It seemed a bit like bonfire night, when you light a firework, then stand well back. All three of them kept well away from the explosive situation and saw little of their parents.

Jane felt very uncomfortable with her new hairstyle, which consisted of a variety of brightly-coloured combs holding her hair in a pile on top of her head. Even Diane despaired in the end when the combs fell out for the hundredth time.

'I give up with your hair, Janey,' Diane sighed, 'though I suppose we could try tying a scarf around it.' She surveyed the wreckage of the new style. 'On second thoughts, we won't bother. You could have it cut really short, I suppose, and . . . .'

'Can't we just forget about my hair? I'd rather just leave it,' Jane told her sister.

'Well, you must admit the make-up is a success—you look tons better,' Diane said, enthusiastically.

As the first week wore on, Diane made friends with a group of teenagers and started to leave Jane on her own at the disco. Jane began to dread it.

'I'm not going to the disco tonight, Di,' she said on the Saturday morning. 'I think I'll go with Mum and Dad to the floor show.'

Diane turned from the mirror where she was liberally applying eye make-up. 'Oh, that's charming! Dad only lets me go because we're together. If you don't come with me, then I can't go. Come on, Jane—don't be so miserable!'

'I don't like sitting on my own,' Jane replied defensively.

'On your own? That's ridiculous! There's hundreds of people there. Just be friendly. Talk to people. Come on, Jane!'

So Jane spent another miserable evening at the disco, wondering why she couldn't enjoy herself like Diane. Why were she and her sister so different?

Towards the end of the holiday, Diane and Jane persuaded Mr Spencer to let them take the bus into the nearby seaside town. When they joined the queue for the bus, they found one of Diane's holiday friends waiting there. They had arranged to meet.

'This is Matthew, Jane,' Diane said, and Matthew put an arm around Diane's shoulders. Jane stared at them. 'We want to spend the day together—OK?'

She went on quickly, before Jane had an opportunity to say anything. 'You'll be all right. Enjoy yourself—look around the shops. We'll meet you back at the bus stop at seven.'

Jane didn't know what to do. 'But what if Dad finds out? We're supposed to stay together.'

'Come on, Jane. Do me a favour! How will he know? Look—here's some extra money. Buy yourself something nice.'

The bus drew in just then, and Diane and Matthew ran upstairs. Jane was forgotten.

She trailed miserably around the town. Trust Diane to get a boyfriend! She found herself wishing *she* had someone. Someone who understood the way she felt . . . thought the same kind of thoughts . . . .

She gazed into shop windows. She bought herself a book and a pair of dangly earrings. She sauntered up and down the promenade, daydreaming. Time passed incredibly slowly.

The seven o'clock bus drew in, but Diane still hadn't arrived. Jane couldn't decide what to do. Should she wait—or go back to Southcoast World by herself?

She waited for the next bus, but still there was no sign of her sister. It was getting late, and they were due back for a family meal at eight.

As she looked anxiously up and down the road, her father's car appeared. He shouted through the open window.

'What the devil are you playing at, young lady? Get in!' His face was red and angry. Had he found out about Diane?

Jane climbed into the car. She'd have to be careful what she said in case she got Diane into trouble.

'Where have you been? Your mother's been frantic! Why weren't you on the seven o'clock bus?'

'I was waiting for Diane.'

'Diane's at home where you should be. What *have* you been doing all this time?'

'Waiting for Diane!' Jane was near to tears.

'But why didn't you catch the bus? You've been mooning about in a dream as usual, I suppose. Wandering off and worrying your sister like that!'

'I didn't wander off. We arranged to meet at seven and I waited for her. She never showed up,' Jane insisted.

'You're the one who didn't show up. You're the one who wandered off. Jane—you're hopeless. Don't you have any sense at all?'

'But Dad! We split up and arranged to meet at seven o'clock. When she didn't turn up I waited for her.'

'Don't whine and make excuses. You didn't split up or arrange anything—you just wandered off in your usual vague fashion. How stupid! Diane was worried, your mother was worried and I had to come out searching for you. We were about to bring in the police to look for you!'

In the confines of the car, Mr Spencer's shouted words were deafening. Jane realised that Diane had been lying.

She opened her mouth to argue—then shut it again. What was the use? If she argued, if she told the truth, he wouldn't believe her. He never did. Whenever there was trouble he always took Diane's side. If Jeremy was involved, Mum always sided with him.

Jane started to cry with anger and frustration. It simply wasn't fair!

'Don't blubber like a baby, girl—I'm not in the mood for it. When we get back, just go to bed. I've had enough hassle from your mother on this holiday to last me the rest of the year.'

Jane did go to bed—without her meal. But when Diane came in, she sat up in bed.

'Why did you lie to Dad, Diane?' she said accusingly. 'I'm sick and tired of always taking the blame for you!'

'What's the big deal? We missed the bus, so we got a taxi back. I thought you would be here already—how was I to know you'd hang about waiting for buses like a wet lettuce? You idiot!'

Diane was furious. 'Because of your stupidity Dad nearly found out about Matthew. How I managed to get lumbered with a fool of a sister like you I don't know.'

Jane turned away. 'I hate you all. You're all selfish pigs!' She sobbed into the pillow.

'Charming,' Diane said sarcastically.

7

'This family is falling apart!'

'Mum's pathetic—she needs to grow up! Listen to her going on at Dad! I don't know why he puts up with it,' Diane said angrily. Mr and Mrs Spencer had been arguing almost every day since their return from holiday.

'Why blame Mum? He's just as bad, swearing and losing his temper all the time,' was Jane's reply.

Diane was putting on her make-up before going out.

'You're not staying in, are you?' Diane remarked. 'Listening to Mum and Dad arguing is enough to drive anybody out of this house. Marriage stinks if you ask me. No fun. All work and rows.'

'I'm babysitting at number four. It's nice and peaceful there, and I get paid. I'm saving up to buy contact lenses. Where are you going?

Diane turned and looked at her sister. 'As a matter of fact, I'm going to a party which just might go on all night. Mum thinks I'm going to Sharon's to sleep—so don't you dare say anything, or I'll kill you!'

Jane looked horrified. 'What if Dad finds out?'

'He won't, will he? And he won't find out about this, either.' She held up a packet of cigarettes.

'You've started smoking? What an idiot! I thought you were keen on being fit and all that,' Jane argued. 'Dad would go spare if he knew.'

'Well, he doesn't know—and he won't.' Diane turned back to her mirror. 'I started smoking on holiday when I was with Matthew. It's not as if I'm hooked on it, or anything. I can stop when I like.'

Jane went on. 'And this party—where is it, and what are you going to be doing all night?'

'Oh, the party's going to be great! It's at Gary Hewitt's—they've got a crate of cider hidden in the cellar and his parents are away, so it'll be brill.'

Diane left and Jane went to her babysitting job.

It was something she really enjoyed doing. It was so peaceful at Martin and Val's. She could watch what she wanted on TV. No one argued or complained. Val always thoughtfully left her a special supper on a tray. It was marvellous to be appreciated so much!

The two children were usually in bed when she arrived, but they always asked for a bedtime story. Getting paid was an extra bonus. Jane enjoyed babysitting so much, she'd have done it for nothing!

As she fell asleep that night she heard her parents arguing again in the next room. She thought of her sister at her all-night party.

'This family is falling apart,' she said to herself, trying to block out the strident, unhappy voices by tucking the bedcovers around her ears.

* * *

The following week, school started again. There was a new timetable and a few new teachers to get used to.

Worst of all, swimming was on their form's timetable for the term. Jane had always disliked games of any kind—but she especially loathed swimming. She couldn't swim, and everybody else could.

For the past year she'd endured hockey, netball and rounders, but she didn't know how she'd survive a weekly visit to the swimming-baths.

'Mum, will you write me a note to say I can't go swimming this week,' Jane asked hopefully.

'Saying what? Why shouldn't you go swimming? It's good for you,' her Mum replied.

'I hate it. Even the smell of the water as I walk through the door is enough to make me sick. Please, Mum—I don't want to go!'

'There's lots of things I don't want to do, but I have to do them. Nobody writes notes to let me off cleaning the mess in this house every night when I come home from work! Goodness knows, your dad spent enough time trying to teach you to swim—Diane and Jeremy learned with no trouble. You'll have to go, Jane. Swimming is part of your education.'

Jane remembered those swimming lessons well, and she felt her stomach clench itself into a tight ball at the memory.

Diane had been the star of *that* show. She was a natural and had quickly learnt to swim and dive.

Jane herself had hated it, though Dad had been patient at first. But Jane was timid, and he'd soon lost patience with her and began to bully and nag. The result was that Jane had never learnt to swim. She knew Dad was convinced she was being awkward and wasn't trying.

Jane felt angry with her mum. She discussed the problem with Mandy on the way to school one day. Mandy had the perfect solution.

'It's simple!' she said. 'Just tell Miss Dickenson you've got a verruca. You don't need a note. If she does ask for one, we'll forge it!'

Miss Dickenson wasn't happy.

'Are you having treatment from the doctor?' she asked Jane.

'No, miss, but I will. The verruca's only just appeared,' Jane replied, feeling guilty.

'Well, see that you do. And next week, bring a verruca-sock to the swimming lesson. They don't cost much.'

Jane's heart sank. Crafty Mandy hadn't thought of that! Sitting on the poolside, Jane realised she was going to have to come up with a better excuse.

* * *

Diane had had a fantastic time at her all-night party. The only sour note had been dancing with a boy who smoked a lot—he had yellow teeth and his breath smelled like an old ashtray!

'It's put me off smoking for life,' she told Jane. 'I'm going to stop!'

The stopping, however, wasn't as easy as she'd thought, and Diane became very irritable. Meanwhile, Mr and Mrs Spencer continued to argue.

One Sunday morning Jane was wakened by raised voices and slamming doors. She sat up listening, reaching for her watch. It was seven-thirty.

She lay down and looked over to where her sister was still sleeping. Nothing woke Diane—she'd sleep through an earthquake. And it sounded like there was one going on in the next room!

Jane tried to read, but she couldn't concentrate. There

was a lot of shouting and banging of cupboards and drawers. She called to her sister.

'What's up?' asked Diane sleepily, sitting up and looking at her clock. 'Good grief—it's the crack of dawn!'

'Listen! Mum and Dad are rowing. It's horrible!'

'Big deal. So what's new?' Diane lay back down.

'But can't we do something? It sounds terrible,' Jane pleaded. 'It sounds like somebody's packing.'

'Well, if it's Mum, good riddance. If it's Dad I'll go with him.' Diane turned over in bed.

Jane went out on to the landing to see what was happening. Jeremy was standing in his doorway, crying. Her parents' bedroom door was open and a suitcase stood at the top of the steps.

Jane walked towards the open door. The room was a shambles. Drawers and cupboards were open and clothes were scattered over the bed and the floor. Mum was sitting on the bed in her dressing-gown. She looked dreadful. Mr Spencer was stuffing socks and underwear into a plastic bag.

Mrs Spencer saw Jane standing in the doorway.

'What are you staring at? Get back to bed!' she snapped.

'Leave it, Pauline. Don't start on the kids. Jane, take your brother downstairs and get yourselves some breakfast.' For a change, Dad spoke quietly.

Jane made Jeremy some toast and tea.

'Dad's a pig,' growled her brother. 'Poor Mum.'

'It takes two to fall out,' Jane said sadly. 'They're as bad as each other as far as I can see.'

Her dad came down the stairs and, without a word, went out of the back door carrying his case. Jane ran upstairs but her mum slammed the bedroom door, shutting her firmly out. She went into her room. Diane was asleep

again.

Jeremy had an asthma attack that morning and had to use his inhaler. Mrs Spencer blamed her husband.

Jane was due to babysit that night for Martin and Val. After a miserable day at home she was looking forward to going. It would be like a calm port after a storm.

'I think I'll get ready to go now,' Jane told her Mum.

'Go where?'

'I'm babysitting for Martin and Val,' Jane said.

'I need you here tonight. You'll have to stay with your brother. I'm going out. It's important.'

'But Mum! I promised!'

Mrs Spencer sighed angrily. 'Then you'll just have to blame your father, won't you? Run down and tell them you can't go.'

Jane was near to tears as she went along to number four. She felt so angry and frustrated. When Val asked her what was wrong, she burst into tears and found herself pouring out the whole story. Val and Martin were understanding and kind. It made Jane cry all the more.

'Don't worry about us,' Val said kindly. 'We'll manage. You go and look after your brother. Help your mum all you can.'

'But you'll miss your night out,' Jane sobbed.

Val smiled, putting her arm around Jane. 'That's nothing. David might do it for us—and if he can't, then we'll just stay home.'

Jane looked up, wiping her eyes. 'David? Do you mean David from across the road?' she asked.

Val nodded. 'He and his family go to our church. He's a super lad. Do you know him?'

'Sort of.'

Jane went home feeling much better. It didn't last,

however. Her mum was feeling very sorry for herself and, as she got ready to go out, was full of bitter complaints about her husband.

'Where are you going, Mum?' Jeremy asked, watching her button her coat.

Mrs Spencer looked at him, tight-lipped. 'It's none of your business,' she said, making for the door.

8

Excuses

'Did I see you talking to Holy Joe at school?' Diane asked her sister.

Jane looked up from her book. 'Who in the world is Holy Joe?'

'That boy, David, from over the road. He's a religious nut. Goes to church all the time—and not just on Sundays!'

'I think he's nice,' Jane said defensively.

'You would. You're a drip,' was Diane's opinion.

Things had been quiet since Dad left. Mum was still irritable, of course, and Jeremy continued to have problems with his asthma, but at least there were no rows.

Swimming loomed on Jane's horizon, but Mandy was always full of bright ideas.

For two weeks the verruca-sock had been conveniently forgotten. The following week she had complained of earache and Mrs Spencer had written a note under protest, saying there would be no more.

'We'll just have to forge a note,' Mandy said. 'What you really need is an excuse that will last for weeks and weeks. Grommets, for example.'

'What on earth are grommets?' Jane asked, laughing.

'Well, my cousin Kelly had these things put in her ears and she couldn't go swimming for about a year. They're like little tubes, I think.'

Jane wasn't convinced. 'You'd need a doctor's note if you weren't going swimming for that long.'

Mandy suddenly had a bright idea.

'Got it!' she cried. 'Go to the doctor and tell him your nerves are bad. Say you come over all peculiar when you go swimming. Tell him the chlorine makes you dizzy, and you panic! There must be a phobia to do with fear of the water. I'll go with you as your witness. It's simple! Make an appointment straightaway.'

'Hang on,' protested Jane. 'I can't go lying to Dr Davidson.'

'You won't be lying completely, will you. Just exaggerating a bit. You hate swimming, right? Don't be so soft!' Mandy was getting annoyed with her friend. 'He'd just write you a note, and that would be that. The only alternative is bunking-off.'

'Bunking-off? Brilliant!' Jane said sarcastically. 'Miss Dickenson's suspicious already. She'd smell fifty thousand rats if I started bunking-off. "Where's Jane Spencer?" she'd ask, and some bright spark would say, "She was here at registration, miss." I can see it all now. I'd really be in for it.'

Jane couldn't decide whether to forge a letter or play truant. She suffered the agony of indecision and didn't sleep very well.

After reading the tragic bits in *Wuthering Heights* yet again, she fell asleep around three.

In the morning she decided she'd tell her mum she felt ill—but was saved the trouble. Jeremy had had a bad night and Mrs Spencer asked Diane and Jane if one of them would stay at home with him so that she could go to work.

'If I lose my job I don't know what we'll do,' she said, a worried frown creasing her brow. 'Your father's done a vanishing trick and the bills still need paying. So it's the only way. Jeremy can't be left in case he has a bad attack.'

Diane shook her head. 'No way! I've got my exams soon and I can't miss classes.'

Jane realised her troubles were over. 'I'll stay with Jeremy—and I'll clean the house and do some washing.'

'You're a dear,' Mrs Spencer said, planting a kiss on Jane's cheek. Then, brushing a tear from her eye, Jane's mum hurried out of the room.

'Aren't we the little Miss Goody-goody,' Diane remarked unkindly.

Jane enjoyed her day at home. She worked hard but still had spare time to watch TV and read. Jeremy was no trouble. He played with his computer in his bedroom and slept for a couple of hours in the afternoon.

Later, Mandy rang.

'I never knew you had it in you—bunking off school,' she said, giggling.

'I didn't. Mum asked me to stay at home because Jeremy's ill. I might not be in school tomorrow, either, with any luck. School's a real pain, anyway.'

Jeremy was ill for a week. The only trouble with being away from school, Jane thought, was that you had to try to catch up with the lessons you missed. Copying from other people's work wasn't easy.

When she arrived back at school the following Monday, she was all ready to hear the news from Mandy.

'Anything interesting happened?' she asked.

'Oh, you're back! Mr Atkinson has been asking about you—I hope you have a good excuse ready. A forged note or a doctor's certificate would do nicely,' Mandy remarked sarcastically.

'What's wrong with you? You know why I haven't been at school. We've got trouble at home and I had to stay with Jeremy. Mum's sent a note explaining.' Jane couldn't understand Mandy's attitude.

'Has she? Big deal!' Mandy said angrily. 'Mr Atkinson *will* be pleased.' She stalked away.

Jane watched her, amazed. What could have happened to make Mandy act that way? She ran after her friend, but Mandy had joined a group of girls and they were staring back at Jane, laughing at what Mandy had just said.

She turned away and went to the form room for registration. She gave the form teacher, Mr Atkinson, the letter from her mum.

'Take this letter to Mrs Saville,' he said curtly. There was an outburst of giggling from where Mandy was sitting.

Jane felt herself turning red. 'Why, sir?' she asked.

'Never mind. Just do it,' Mr Atkinson told her, beginning to mark the register.

Mrs Saville was the head of year. She was a formidable woman and Jane felt nervous as she went along the corridor to her office.

'Come!' Mrs Saville's voice boomed in answer to Jane's timid knock.

'Ah—Jane Spencer! You're back, are you?' She peered at Jane over her half-moon spectacles. 'I'm afraid I've been hearing stories about you.'

Jane's stomach lurched. What on earth was happening? First, Mandy acting strangely, now Mrs Saville.

'Mr Atkinson asked me to bring you this note.' Jane handed it over, her hand trembling as she did so.

Mrs Saville read the letter. 'Well, this seems genuine.'

'I don't understand,' Jane said timidly.

Mrs Saville took off her glasses and stared at Jane. Her cold grey eyes flashed. X-ray eyes, Jane thought, like Superman's.

'Mr Atkinson says you've been forging notes. Is that true? What have you got to say for yourself?'

Jane gulped and blushed. Her mouth went dry and her hands felt icy-cold yet clammy.

'No, Mrs Saville. I haven't,' Jane said in a shaky voice.

'Well, we'll leave it there. But any notes you bring in future I want to see personally.'

Mrs Saville nodded at Jane and put her glasses back on, adding, in a softer voice, 'I'm sorry to hear about your trouble at home, Jane.' She returned to her writing.

The bell rang and Jane hurried to her first lesson where she found Mandy sitting with someone else and looking very pleased with herself.

Had Mandy told lies about her to get her into trouble? Admittedly, Jane had thought about forging notes for swimming but she'd never actually done it. She spent a miserable day at school without her friend's company.

That evening the mystery of Mandy's behaviour was solved. Jane was telling Diane what had happened.

'She's probably annoyed because you've pinched her heart-throb,' Diane declared. 'Mandy Giddins is a sneaking tell-tale like her brother and sister. You're well rid of her as a friend.'

'Pinched her heart-throb? What do you mean?' Jane asked, amazed.

'David, the religious fruit-cake. She was asking me about him the other day and I said you and he were as thick as thieves, that's all.'

Diane shrugged. 'She seemed very annoyed. But don't

worry about her—you don't need her!' With that, Diane left the room.

So that was it. All was explained. Mandy was annoyed because of what Diane had told her, and to get her own back she'd lied to Mr Atkinson about the forged notes.

Jane felt terrible. She'd lost a friend because of her sister's stupid remarks and her friend had displayed her true colours. School was bad enough, but without Mandy it was going to be awful.

The final blow came when Jane remembered it was swimming tomorrow.

9

Who cares?

'Jane Spencer, you are the limit!' Miss Dickenson yelled.

Jane winced and her heart did leapfrogs in her chest.

'You've come for six weeks with your lame excuses. We've had verrucas, earaches and headaches. Last week you weren't even here. And now you have the cheek to tell me your nerves are bad and you haven't had time to see the doctor!'

The teacher's voice was harsh and loud. The girls in the corridor giggled and Jane wished the ground would open up and swallow her.

'It's *my* nerves, not yours, that are under stress, coping with stupid girls like you. *You are going swimming.* Line up over there for the bus.' Miss Dickenson walked away.

'But, miss!' Jane protested. 'I haven't brought my things.'

The PE teacher turned around and glared at her.

'I'm well prepared for that excuse, Jane Spencer. I have a supply of spare costumes and towels, so get in line, now! You, my girl, are going swimming.'

Jane felt sick as the bus made its way through the busy traffic to the local swimming-baths. The smell of the chlorine made her worse. The triumphant look on Mandy's face hurt her deeply, and she verged on crying.

It was a nightmare. She was the only person in the shallow end and many of the girls splashed her and made unkind comments. Mandy conspired with two other girls to try and duck her under the water, but Miss Dickenson always seemed to be around when they were anywhere near Jane.

'Relax, girl. You'll never learn to swim hanging on to the side like grim death. Let your legs come up. Jane—let them come up! Now how about some leg strokes? Put your chin into the water.'

Miss Dickenson turned away tutting and Jane was relieved to be left alone. Later, in the changing-room, the dam finally broke when she discovered someone had hidden her panties. She burst into tears and Miss Dickenson made everyone search for them till they reappeared.

Back at school Jane ate her lunch alone. That night she couldn't get to sleep. Whenever she closed her eyes she was reliving her experience at the baths. How could she face the next swimming lesson? Perhaps she really *should* see the doctor?

The next evening she went round to babysit for Val and Martin. Whenever she went into their house she felt better—she didn't know why. They were so friendly and kind it made her feel happy, yet at the same time she wanted to cry.

She watched Val hug and kiss her children as she put them to bed. Jane couldn't remember being treated like that when she was little.

There was nothing interesting on TV so she read the book she'd got from the library earlier that day. It was written by a mother whose teenage daughter had died of leukaemia. Jane always looked for the sad books!

Laurie, the girl in the book, had been pretty and gifted—then, at the age of sixteen, was struck down with the terrible disease.

When she first began to lose weight she was glad—she'd always wanted a slender figure, and now it was happening without any effort. But when she began to complain of constant tiredness, her mother insisted on a visit to the doctor.

He sent her immediately for hospital tests—and Laurie's fight for life began. The book told of the girl's courage, and the way the whole family's lifestyle was changed by her illness. Jane's eyes flew over the pages with dread.

Laurie had lost a lot of weight. So had she.

Laurie had been constantly pale and tired. So was she!

By the time Jane had read the first few chapters she was convinced that she, too, had leukaemia.

She lay on Val's couch and sobbed. 'I might as well be dead,' she thought.

Her mum and dad couldn't care less about her. Diane and Jeremy were leading their own selfish lives. Would any of them care if she *did* have leukaemia? Maybe they'd all be sorry when she died from it. She pictured Mandy and the other girls at school, wishing they'd treated her differently.

When Val and Martin came back, Jane couldn't stop crying. Martin went to make a cup of tea and Val put an arm around her shoulders.

'What's wrong, Jane?' she asked, kindly. 'Tell me.'

'I think I've got leukaemia,' Jane blurted out. She passed the book to Val, choking on a sob.

Val glanced at the back cover. 'You've read the book, and now you think you've got leukaemia. Is that it?'

Jane nodded. Val put the book down.

'I'm always tired and that seems to be the main symptom. I'm so scared,' Jane muttered. Val comforted her, stroking her head.

'Jane, you're not ill—you're unhappy. The reason you feel tired is because you're miserable and worried all the time.'

'How did you know I was unhappy?' Jane asked, beginning to calm down.

'Well, we care about you. We've been praying for you.'

Jane looked at Val in amazement. She liked Val and Martin a lot, but she'd had no idea they cared about her.

She thought again about her parents. They didn't care, not really. Jane was always second best with both of them. Diane was Dad's favourite, and Mum seemed to prefer Jeremy.

'It's good to know *somebody* cares!' Jane said shakily, wiping her eyes.

'I know somebody who not only cares, but loves you and wants to change your life—God!'

Martin came in at that moment, carrying a tray with a teapot, mugs and a jug of milk.

'I wish something could change me,' Jane told him. 'I'm so miserable—at home, at school—everywhere. I hate myself for being like that, but I can't seem to do anything about it!'

'I used to be just like you,' Val said, pouring out the tea. 'I was always depressed and down in the dumps. I felt ugly and unwanted. As far as I was concerned, I was one of life's losers! Then my friend told me about God. She said he loved me and wanted me to belong to him. She told me how he could change my life completely.'

Jane blew her nose. 'I can't imagine you being

miserable,' she said, sipping gratefully from her mug of tea. 'I've never thought much about God. I used to go to Sunday school when I was a little girl, but it was dead boring.' She put her head in her hands.

'Look—why don't you come to tea tomorrow and we'll talk some more?' Martin suggested. 'It's very late and your mum will be wondering where you are.'

Mrs Spencer was asleep in front of the television. Even in her sleep a worried frown creased her forehead, and Jane felt suddenly sorry for her mum. Mrs Spencer woke up suddenly, rubbing her eyes.

'Shall I make a hot drink, Mum?' Jane asked.

'Oh, yes please, Jane. I don't know how long I've been asleep. Diane isn't in yet. I wish she wouldn't stay out so late. I hope she isn't going into pubs.'

'Mum?' Jane asked later as they sipped their hot chocolate. 'Do you ever think about God?'

'God?' Mrs Spencer laughed. 'What about him?'

'I just wondered what you thought about him. Did you ever go to church?'

'I did when I was young. That's where I met your dad—at the church youth group. Once we started courting, though, we didn't bother going anymore. Church is all right if you like that kind of thing, but it's a bit dismal, if you ask me.'

'Val and Martin go to church, and they're not dismal. Just the opposite! They seem to have something special .... I don't know quite how to explain it.'

'Well, bully for them,' Mrs Spencer said, cynically. 'I wish I had something special. All I've got at the moment are bills I can't pay, a sick son and a husband who's done a runner!' She stood up. 'Come on, let's go to bed.'

Diane didn't come in until after midnight and Jane heard

the rise and fall of angry voices through the bedroom wall. Diane was in a bad temper when she finally came into their bedroom.

'Stupid old bat,' she said. 'Nag, nag, nag. No wonder Dad went off! I'm nearly sixteen, and a late night here and there isn't going to hurt.'

'She's worried about you. Wondering what you're up to. She thinks you've been going into pubs. She's got enough to worry about without you upsetting her.'

'So, what if I have been into pubs? Why shouldn't I? Who cares? Certainly not Dad—he's gone off and left us, and Mum only cares about her precious Jeremy and his wonky chest. So I've stopped caring about *them.* They're pathetic. Me, I care about me. I'll do what I want to do, and nobody's going to stop me.'

Diane jumped into bed and turned out the light. 'So, little sister, shut up and go to sleep.'

Jane turned over and pulled the covers around her shoulders. 'Doesn't anybody in this family care about anybody else?' she wondered. Even Diane sounded miserable. Diane—her attractive, gifted sister.

'But God cares,' she whispered into the darkness just before she fell into a deep, dreamless sleep.

10

Police!

'Here is the news. Jane Specky Four-eyes, alias Twiggy, has been chosen to represent her country in the Olympic seven-mile butterfly stroke race.'

Shaun McSpadden made his announcement in a BBC voice as Jane walked into registration next morning. Jane blushed and hurried to her seat. Mandy and her friends giggled.

'Here is a newsflash. Here is a newsflash,' Shaun shouted. 'Yesterday, Jane Spencer lost her knickers at the baths and cried like a baby.'

'Thank you, McSpadden. That's quite enough,' Mr Atkinson barked as he came into the room to mark the register. 'Now sit down and shut up.'

But Shaun McSpadden didn't shut up at all that morning, and Mandy and her friends kept up their laughing and giggling.

By lunch-time Jane felt like running home. As she ate her lunch alone, trying to hide behind a group of sixth-form boys, she heard someone call her name. Her heart sank.

'Hi, Jane. Can I join you?'

Jane didn't look up. 'Bog off, McSpadden! Go and boil

your fat head,' she said—then glanced up. David stood there holding his lunch-tray and staring at her in amazement.

Scarlet with embarrassment, Jane leapt to her feet. All she wanted to do was rush away! But when she saw Mandy and her friends staring at her, she sat down again quickly.

'Are you all right, Jane?' David asked, concerned. 'Having trouble from big-mouth McSpadden?'

'I'm OK, thanks,' Jane replied. The look of jealousy on Mandy's face made her feel slightly better. She found herself telling David about the swimming-baths, and about Mandy and her mean tricks.

'Just ignore her,' David advised. 'If she sees you're upset she'll do it all the more. Try laughing! Go on—let's see you smile.'

Jane smiled. She couldn't help it. And it was such a relief after her terrible morning that she began to laugh.

Mandy looked furious and stormed out of the dining-room in such a rush that she bumped straight into Mr Atkinson, who was on dinner duty, sending his tray of food crashing to the floor. The teacher made Mandy fetch a mop and bucket and clean the floor. Jane was helpless with laughter. It was infectious, and David joined in.

After that, she felt she could face the afternoon—if things got difficult she could survive by picturing Mandy with her mop!

'We're having a barbecue on Saturday. Would you like to come?' David asked when all the hilarity had died down.

Immediately, Jane felt her tenseness returning, and she heard herself saying, 'Sorry, I can't.'

Why couldn't she be friendly and relaxed? As she walked to her first lesson she felt like kicking herself.

After school, Jane hurried home to change, looking

forward to the meal at Val and Martin's. She looked for David, but didn't see him. All afternoon she'd been rehearsing a speech, telling him she'd changed her mind and would like to go to the barbecue after all.

Jane helped Val in the kitchen, crawled around the floor with Peter and Laura and listened to Martin's seemingly endless stock of corny jokes. She had a marvellous time!

'I love coming here,' she gasped, weak with laughter. 'I've never met anyone like you two before. You're so—*different!*'

Martin wiggled his eyebrows. 'Is that an insult or a compliment?'

'You know what I mean. You're *nice!*'

'We weren't always nice,' Val said seriously. 'But I told you that yesterday, didn't I?'

Jane shook her head. 'I still can't believe it.'

'That's because God's changed us both so much.'

Jane looked puzzled.

'You wouldn't imagine, for instance, that I had a drink problem when I was a teenager,' Martin said.

Jane shook her head slowly, thunderstruck.

'I started going into pubs with my mates when I was sixteen. At first, I'd just have the odd beer—but before long I found I had a liking for it. In the end, I could drink them all under the table. A guy in the office where I worked realised I had a problem, but it was a long time before I swallowed my pride and admitted it.

'This guy was a Christian—he used to talk to me about how Jesus wanted to set me free and give me a new kind of life.'

'And that made you different?'

Martin nodded, grinning. 'But not until I was really willing to change. God doesn't force himself on us. I found out for myself that this friend of mine was right. God *does* care.'

'He cares about you, too, Jane,' put in Val. 'He sent his Son to die for you. He wants you to be his child.'

Martin took a well-thumbed Bible from the bookshelf and turned the pages. 'Listen to what Jesus said, Jane.' He found the words he was looking for and read them aloud. ' "He has sent me to proclaim freedom for the prisoners and recovery of sight for the blind, to release the oppressed," ' he read.

Jane listened, feeling like that prisoner, oppressed and hurt—trapped inside her own problems. Had Jesus really come to set her free? Her lip trembled.

'I wish I could believe *somebody* cares about me,' she whispered. 'My sister, Diane, has always been Daddy's darling and Mum thinks there's nobody in the world like her Jeremy! When I was born, she wanted a boy—she told me so. That really hurts, and as I get older it seems to hurt more. I'm nobody's favourite—I'm second best!'

'You're not second best in God's eyes, though,' Val said with feeling.

'But I'm useless at just about everything,' Jane went on. 'Diane's got the brains as well as the looks. I'm not as intelligent as she is—she's brilliant at school. And as for sport, I'm so hopeless I can't even swim. I know it's ridiculous, but I'm scared stiff of water!'

'I couldn't swim, either, when I was your age,' Val confessed. 'I was petrified as soon as I got anywhere near water. But God helped me. He took away my fear and I learned to swim on my eighteenth birthday.

'Look, I'll teach you to swim if you like. We could go to the baths on Monday evening. It's ladies only after eight o'clock, so it's nice and quiet. We'll soon have you swimming!'

Val sounded so confident. Jane was excited—but scared at the same time. Was it all too good to be true?

Before she left, Martin and Val invited her to the barbecue on Saturday night. So she would see David there after all!

It was nearly eleven when she arrived home—but Diane was still out. As she apologised for being late, Jane could see her mum was worried.

'At least I know where you've been for the evening,' she said. 'Those people might be religious fanatics, but it's harmless stuff.'

'Mum, they're not religious fanatics. Martin and Val are really nice people,' Jane protested.

Her mum laughed. 'Well, I don't mind you going there as long as they don't try to brainwash you! You're silly enough to believe anything!'

Jane's heart sank into her shoes, and she felt the familiar knot of tension tighten up inside her. She wanted to run back to the peace of Martin and Val's.

Suddenly, there was a loud knocking on the door and Jane and her mum jumped and looked fearfully into each other's eyes. Mrs Spencer peeped through the curtains.

'Oh, no,' she gasped. 'It's the police!' She sank, trembling, into a chair. 'Jane—go and answer the door.' Even her lips were pale.

Jane opened the door and a policewoman said something that Jane didn't hear. She stared in amazement at the police car. Diane was sitting in the back seat, her nose pressed against the window. She was waving and had a glazed expression and a feeble grin on her face.

The policewoman touched Jane's arm. 'Are your parents in?'

Jane dragged her eyes from her sister and apologised. 'I'm sorry. Yes, Mum's in.'

'Can I have a word, please?' the policewoman said.

Diane was drunk. She and her friends had been messing about in someone's garden pond and the police had been called. After keeping her some time at the police station, they had brought her home.

Jane watched as her sister was helped into the house. She was sick in the hall, then staggered through to the kitchen. Jane heard her being sick again, and shuddered. Mrs Spencer stood very still as the police talked to her. They had decided merely to give a caution, not to press drunk and disorderly charges.

When they had gone, Diane wove her way to the sofa and sat down heavily, her face the colour of old cheese. Her mother stood on the hearth-rug, staring at her oldest daughter. She was shaking with suppressed anger.

'Go to bed, Mother. It's no big deal,' Diane muttered, holding her head in her hands. 'Just leave me here to die.' She fell over sideways on the sofa, groaning.

Mrs Spencer exploded.

She shot forward, screaming and shouting. She swore and called Diane names. She began to hit her around the head and shoulders as she sobbed and yelled.

Jane was horrified. She tried to grab her mother and received a stinging slap across the face.

'Get to bed, Jane!' her mum shouted as she turned again on Diane, who was sobbing and covering her head with her arms.

'How will I ever face the neighbours again?' she gasped, lashing out at Diane.

And then it was over. Mrs Spencer dissolved into tears and ran from the room, sobbing.

Jeremy was standing at the bottom of the stairs in his pyjamas, bleary-eyed and afraid.

'What's wrong, Mum?' he asked.

'Oh, my poor sweetheart! I didn't mean to wake you! Are you all right?' She put her arms around him and led him back upstairs.

In the sudden quiet, Jane stood, hurting inside, tears coursing down her face. What a place! What a family! Diane, fast asleep on the sofa, snored loudly.

Jane turned off the television and put out the light. She locked the front door and slowly climbed the stairs to bed, feeling as though she had been through a mincing-machine.

Then she remembered what Val had told her. God cared about her. He loved her.

Was it really true?

11

Adolf's antics

The next morning, Diane didn't go to school. She had a hangover and lay in bed, her glazed eyes reminding Jane of an anaemic codfish on a fishmonger's slab.

'I feel like death warmed up,' she moaned as Jane was dressing. 'Get me some paracetamol, Jane. And do turn off the light—it's hurting my eyes! My tongue feels disgusting—like a piece of old carpet!'

Diane pulled the sheet over her head, groaning. 'Oh, my eyes!'

Jane wished she didn't have to go to school. The thought of facing Mandy and her friends again made her feel almost as bad as her sister.

Shaun McSpadden had what, to him, was a good day. He took his pet mouse, Adolf, to school, hidden inside his jumper.

In the classroom that morning he and Adolf caused quite a stir. And as Shaun went from lesson to lesson, the teachers couldn't quite make out what was wrong with form three-ten. The girls, especially, they commented later in the staffroom, seemed to be acting oddly—at times bordering on hysteria.

Jane was pleased about the mouse. Everyone was fully occupied with what Adolf was doing, and left her alone. Mandy hated mice and worried herself into hysterics, and Shaun was too busy even to look at Jane. It was good to be without his stupid remarks.

At lunch-time, David sat with Jane again in the dining-room.

'What's going on over there?' he asked as he put his tray down next to Jane's.

'It's McSpadden. He's brought his pet mouse to school and some of the girls are going spare!' Jane told him. 'It's quite a cute little mouse really, but it can't be very bright or it wouldn't stay with Shaun McSpadden. Living down his jumper can't be very nice for the poor little thing.'

Adolf may not have been bright but he was certainly adventurous. The mouse decided to explore further afield. Suddenly, he shot to the floor and ran across the dining-room. When he moved, he moved fast—and so did the girls when they saw him heading their way.

Wherever Adolf went, Shaun McSpadden wasn't far behind. He, too, was a quick mover.

Dinners, drinks and cutlery crashed to the floor as Adolf explored the dining-room. Chairs overturned, people shouted and laughed, and Shaun did an impression of a rugby player trying desperately, against all odds, to retrieve the ball.

Some of the boys joined in with enthusiasm, diving at Adolf, who darted, like greased lightning, this way and that. The panic was infectious, and girls climbed on to chairs and tables screaming and clutching their skirts.

Mr Atkinson stood at the end of the hall looking grim. In one hand he held a dish of jam roly-poly and custard. With his other hand he fumbled for his whistle. Putting

the whistle to his lips, he blew a long, ear-piercing blast, his cheeks turning red and his eyes popping.

Silence reigned. Shaun stood up, very dishevelled, clutching Adolf, who looked none the worse for wear.

Mr Atkinson took a deep breath and everyone winced in anticipation of his acid comments. Suddenly, Mandy, who was standing near him, fainted, going down like a felled tree. The teacher watched in horror as his dish of roly-poly flew out of his hand, neatly tipping yellow custard down his suit and then landing upside down on the floor.

He sighed heavily. Jam roly-poly was his favourite pudding—and he'd just been given the last piece of it.

'That dratted girl again,' he said, looking down at Mandy's prostrate form lying at his feet. 'Clear up!' he yelled, striding over her and out of the dining-room, leaving a long trail of custard behind him.

Two other teachers hurried forward to give first-aid to Mandy, and everyone began to tidy things up—except Shaun McSpadden, who sat at his table gently stroking his pet mouse.

Shaun was sent home with Adolf, and Mandy was collected by her mum. The rest of the afternoon was quiet and uneventful.

That evening Jane called round at Val's to confirm that she would like to go to the barbecue. Val was blow-drying her hair.

'You're clever,' said Jane admiringly. 'I wish I knew how to do my hair—I hate mine.'

'I was a hairdresser before I had the children,' Val told her, surprisingly. 'If you come round tomorrow afternoon, I'll do your hair for you before we go to the barbecue.'

Jane was thrilled and excited at the prospect.

At home, however, things were neither thrilling nor

exciting. Mum wasn't speaking to Diane, and Diane was sulky and morose. She was to stay home in the evenings and was very depressed about it. Jeremy wasn't well and, as usual, expected everyone to be his willing slave.

* * *

Jane woke up on Saturday morning feeling good. She wished she could always feel this way.

In the afternoon she went round to Val's and found her on her own. Martin had taken the children out to the playground.

Val shampooed and blow-dried Jane's hair. She had the professional hairdresser's knack of making it look really special, and Jane gasped as she looked in the mirror.

'Val! I don't know what to say—it's fantastic!'

They drank coffee and talked about clothes and make-up and what colours suited Jane best. Val knew all about skin care and gave Jane some cleansing lotion and showed her how to use it.

They also talked about getting enough sleep and eating the right foods.

'When you're a teenager you need plenty of fresh fruit and vegetables and crispy salads,' Val told Jane. 'Cut down on fatty foods like fish and chips and chocolate. Drink plenty of water.'

Jane felt very special, and she hummed happily to herself as she washed up the coffee-cups. She looked again at the poster on the kitchen wall.

' "He cares for you." ' She read the words aloud.

She was beginning to believe it.

12

Some things can change

It was a perfect evening for a barbecue. Wisps of thin grey smoke floated over the large secluded garden. Delicious smells of sizzling chicken and sausages, onions and burgers, hung on the air.

David took Jane round and introduced her to so many people she felt quite overwhelmed. But everyone was friendly, and Jane found her nervousness slowly evaporating.

She had always imagined Christians as serious and solemn, and that church was full of old ladies. But here she was surrounded by laughing teenagers having fun!

Val was serving salad and Jane gravitated back to her. She felt somehow safe with Val.

'Hi there!' Jane recognised the girl who spoke to her. She was a fifth-former from school. 'I'm Michelle. Are you David's friend?'

'Yes—this is Jane Spencer,' Val told her. 'Why don't you go and sit down, girls? It's not easy to eat standing up.'

Michelle and Jane sat down with their meal.

'I've seen you around,' Michelle said, tackling a chicken leg. Juice ran down her chin and the two girls laughed.

'You're Diane's sister, aren't you?'

Jane nodded. She felt awkward, as usual, talking to strangers, but she needn't have worried. Michelle was friendly and relaxed and soon they were chatting like old friends.

'Your hair's looking nice tonight. That style suits you,' Michelle told her admiringly.

'Oh, thanks.' Jane blushed. 'Val did it for me. She used to be a hairdresser. My hair was such a mess before—she's done wonders.'

'You babysit for Val and Martin, don't you? Aren't their kids cute? Especially the little one!'

'They're a great family,' Jane told her. 'They've really helped me. Val is teaching me to swim.' Immediately, Jane wished she hadn't mentioned the swimming lessons—Michelle would think her a dummy, not being able to swim at her age. But Michelle didn't laugh. She seemed genuinely sympathetic.

'That's great. I love swimming. Maybe I'll come along and give you moral support.'

Soon the girls were chatting about school, then they went for second helpings.

'Why don't you come to our meeting on Sunday morning?' Michelle asked. 'I'll meet you if you like.'

Suddenly, Jane was shy and awkward again.

'I don't know,' she replied, scarlet with embarrassment. 'I wouldn't fit in. I can't be like Val and Martin. I'm hopeless at things. I don't think I'm strong enough to be a Christian. I'd fail.'

'You don't have to be strong, Jane,' Michelle said suddenly. 'Jesus is strong enough—and that's all that matters! He loves you just as you are. To him you're unique and special.'

Jane didn't feel unique or special. She felt worthless. Even her own parents thought she was useless! She was third-rate, second best. Plain Jane.

Michelle went on. 'You needn't feel hopeless any longer, Jane. And you don't have to worry about changing yourself, either. God helps with the changing when we accept him into our lives. He makes us his children—part of his family.'

'Come on, you two—coffee's being served over here,' David called above the babble of voices, and Jane and Michelle joined the queue of people waiting for drinks.

Jane leaned on the garden fence and looked over into the next garden, deep in thought. The houses in the road were large Victorian semis and some had been made into flats. A man came out of one of the flats and Jane immediately shrank back, her heart hammering. The man was her father! He turned the corner of the house and disappeared.

'Jane, do you want coffee or tea?' her new friend asked. Michelle turned and saw Jane's face. 'Are you all right?' she asked.

'I've just seen my dad coming out of the house next door,' Jane replied without thinking. 'It was a bit of a shock—he left home a few weeks ago and we didn't know where he was.'

'Oh, Jane, I'm sorry,' Michelle said kindly.

'I wonder whether I should tell Mum?' Jane sighed. Seeing her father again had brought back the old tensions.

When Jane went home she hoped her family would notice her new hairstyle and ask about the barbecue. Diane was watching TV, a rebellious scowl on her face. Mrs Spencer was looking very determined and the atmosphere of anger and resentment was a big contrast to the relaxed, happy time she'd spent at the barbecue.

'You'd better smell Jane's breath, Mother,' Diane said bitterly. 'After all, she may have been to the pub. You can't afford to trust her, you know.' She continued to stare fixedly at the TV.

Jane sighed, sensing a row.

Mrs Spencer snapped back, 'You're the one who can't be trusted. But don't worry—I'll be watching you, my girl. You won't shame me again. When I fid out where your father is, you can join him. He's always spoilt you, made you think you were the bee's knees. Well, I'm not putting up with your clever ways.'

'If he has any sense he won't ever turn up again. And if I knew where he was I'd love to join him. Anywhere would be better than here, where my nagging, mean mother never gives it a rest,' Diane said, her voice growing shrill.

Jane wanted to run out of the room, jam her fingers in her ears—anything to get away from the noise of anger and hate.

Before long they were both yelling at each other, TV commercials adding their contribution to the din.

The door swung open slowly and Jeremy stood there in his pyjamas. His face was chalk-white, his huge, frightened eyes staring wildly around the room. His chest was heaving, his mouth wide open as he fought for breath.

There was a sudden silence, and they all heard the harsh rasping of his throat and lungs. The boy's eyes rolled upwards and he staggered, then fell into a pathetic heap on the living-room floor.

Diane stared in horror as her mother screamed and ran forward. Jane ran out of the room and up the stairs, taking them two at a time.

'God, please help us!' she gasped. She ran into Jeremy's room and began searching on his bedside table for his inhaler. It was lying by his pillow. She grabbed it and ran.

'God! Don't let him die!'

Her mother snatched the inhaler from her. Jane looked down at her brother's pinched, waxen face and knew what she must do. She flew to the phone and dialled 999.

Diane stood fearfully in the middle of the living-room, like someone turned to stone.

Mrs Spencer was frantic. She began to call her husband's name as she knelt on the floor trying to revive her son. Jane came in and dragged Diane out of the room. She shook her sister hard.

'Diane—go to the gate and watch for the ambulance. When you see it coming, wave like mad to show them where to come.'

'I can't bear illness!' Diane wailed. 'This can't be happening!'

Jane shoved her out of the front door. 'Do it!' she ordered. 'Go on.'

Mrs Spencer looked up at Jane. 'If only I knew where to find your father,' she said dementedly.

'I know where he is,' Jane told her. 'I'll get him and bring him to the hospital.'

Jane turned and ran out of the house and down the street to Martin and Val's. The house was all in darkness.

'Please, God, help me!'

She rang the doorbell again and again. A light went on upstairs, and Martin appeared at the window. When he saw Jane he waved and disappeared. As he opened the door Jane saw, with relief, the ambulance coming down the street. Her sister was out on the pavement, waving furiously.

'It's my brother,' Jane gasped. 'He's having a bad asthma attack! I sent for the ambulance. I've got to fetch my dad—he's living in a flat next door to where the barbecue was. Will you please take me there?'

Martin didn't hesitate. He was dressed in two minutes and was starting up the car. Val put her arms around Jane. 'God will help you and your family,' she said.

'I know he will,' Jane called over her shoulder as she climbed into the car.

There was a light on in the house, and Mr Spencer was soon located.

'Thanks, mate,' he said, as they arrived at the hospital's emergency unit. He was soon running up the drive.

'Martin, thanks so much.' Jane turned to leave.

'Anytime, Jane. I'm glad I could help.'

Before she closed the car door, Jane hesitated. 'Would you give Michelle a message for me, please?' she said. 'Tell her I'd like to go to the church meeting on Sunday after all. I'll give her a ring when this is all over.'

'That's great, Jane,' Martin said enthusiastically.

Jane smiled. 'I've been thinking about what Michelle said at the barbecue—that God loves me just as I am.'

Martin nodded. 'She's right—he does! And the Bible says that anyone becoming a Christian is a new creation. Old things are past and everything becomes new!'

'I must dash, Martin. See you later. And thanks again!'

Jane hurried away up the drive, wondering what to expect. She asked at the reception desk about her brother, and a nurse took her through into Casualty.

'He's out of danger, love. Don't look so worried,' the nurse said reassuringly.

She opened the curtains into one of the cubicles—and Jane breathed a sigh of relief.

Jeremy was propped up on pillows and covered with a bright-red blanket. He had an oxygen mask over his mouth, and he looked very pale under his freckles—but he was breathing normally. That terrible grating, gasping noise had stopped.

He raised his hand to her. 'Hi, Sparrow-legs,' he said weakly.

Jane smiled. He was going to be all right.

Her mum and dad were standing very close together by Jeremy's bed. Mrs Spencer put an arm around Jane's shoulder and hugged her.

'Jane—you were marvellous!' she said huskily. 'I don't know what I'd have done without you tonight.'

Jane's mouth dropped open and she stared at her mother, amazed.

'Yes, well done, our Jane,' her dad added kindly. 'They're taking Jeremy up to the ward soon—they'll be keeping him here for observation, at least until tomorrow.'

He cleared his throat. 'Look, Jane—your mum and I need to talk. Will you stay here with Jeremy for a few minutes?'

The 'few minutes' turned into an hour—but when they came back after their talk, they were holding hands. Jane's dad told her he was coming back home for good.

Mrs Spencer elected to stay with Jeremy overnight at the hospital. He was now sleeping peacefully. Jane and her father took a taxi home.

'It's a good thing you saw me when you were at that barbecue, Jane,' her dad said as they went into the house. 'Your mum's told me what Diane's been up to. Where is she? I want to get things sorted out.'

He called up the stairs. 'Diane, are you there? We're back. Jeremy's going to be all right. Come down—I want to talk to you about what you've been up to.'

Jane passed her sister on the stairs. 'Nothing changes,' Diane said, trying to look unconcerned.

Jane went into her bedroom. She closed the door but could still hear her dad shouting and Diane's sulky, defiant replies.

'Oh, God,' she prayed, remembering the bit from the Bible that Martin had told her. 'I want to be a new creation. I want everything to become new for me.'

She spotted *Wuthering Heights* by her pillow as she got into bed. She picked the book up and shoved it right to the back of the nearest cupboard.

She snuggled down under the covers, listening to the row as it continued downstairs. Some things didn't change.

'But other things do,' Jane whispered. She would be a Christian, a new creation.

'I'll tell David about it tomorrow,' she murmured as she fell asleep.